STRESS
In The Workplace-
How To
Cause It

Howard Edwards

NEW
HOLLAND

First published in 2003 by
New Holland Publishers (UK) Ltd
London • Cape Town • Sydney • Auckland
www.newhollandpublishers.com

Garfield House
86-88 Edgware Road
London W2 2EA, United Kingdom

80 McKenzie Street
Cape Town 8001, South Africa

Level 1, Unit 4
Suite 411, 14 Aquatic Drive
Frenchs Forest, NSW 2086, Australia

218 Lake Road
Northcote, Auckland, New Zealand

2 4 6 8 10 9 7 5 3 1

ISBN 1 84330 519 4

Editor: Gareth Jones
Editorial Direction: Rosemary Wilkinson
Designer: Paul Wright
Production: Lucy Hulme

Reproduction by Pica Digital, Singapore
Printed and bound by Times Offset (M) Sdn Bhd, Malaysia

DISCLAIMER

*The Author and The Publisher and its Agents and Vendors accept no responsibility
whatsoever for any ill health, injuries or fatalities arising from, or related to,
usage of this book.*

ACKNOWLEDGMENTS

Mental anguish is the precursor of productivity and I am grateful to my publishers, New Holland, for engendering an extraordinarily stressful environment, in which, for once, I receive more than I give and which allows this book to be the child of Pressure and Anxiety. So, reluctant and somewhat fearful thanks must go to the following:

Rosemary, my Publishing Manager, for her authoritarian rule, which made writing this book so intensely painful, and for allowing me to reap the benefits of destructive criticism and editorial rejection. Gareth, my Editor, for unsettling my mind and introducing me to the pressure of arbitrary deadlines and isolation, all of which have had a commendably deleterious effect on my confidence. Lucy, my Production Controller, for her unrelenting ambushes with unreasonable demands, which continue to cause discomfort and doubt bordering on paranoia. Sandy, for threatening to withhold payment and for taking demoralization and insecurity to new depths, while ensuring that pure abuse reaches new heights. Yvonne, my Publicist, for her constant criticism and for inflicting unbearable pressure and distress coupled with an alarm born of physical intimidation. Catherine and Adam, for their inspirational endeavours to make me the victim of ritual humiliation, while helping to maintain an environment of wall-to-wall stress. Brian, Colin, Don, Howard, Jackie, Katie and Ted for their individual efforts in ensuring I remain ridden with top quality hypertension, painfully and permanently hovering on the brink of failure and professional ruin. And last, but most certainly not least, Alexandra, for subjugating me to the point of tyranny, while showing me that I can take more fear, anguish and stress than I thought a mortal could bear.

Howard Edwards

FOREWORD

This book explodes the myth that a happy company is a productive one. It shows how to avoid the complacency and inefficiency that follow a sense of well-being and job security. Too many business books focus on employee contentment and team building without acknowledging that the feel-good factor this engenders actually makes a business more placid and therefore less competitive. So, this book is premised on the observation that stress, at what could be considered an unacceptable level, has a vital role to play in a company's success.

Stress in the Workplace is full of inventive and imaginative ways to ensure that your colleagues perform to their full potential and that your work environment is bereft of comfort and languor. This isn't an instant solution to all your challenges but, in the dynamics of a vibrant workplace in need of breakthrough initiatives, some of the benefits will be immediate. Anxious people produce answers, and this is a complete strategy for creating and managing a more productive and profitable organisation in a stressful environment.

CONTENTS

Chapter 1
A Brief History Of Stress

THE ROLE OF STRESS IN EVOLUTION

Locke, in a rare moment of relaxation, said, "Though the faculties of the mind are improved by exercise, yet they must not be put to a stress beyond their strength." In his careful use of the word "beyond", Locke reveals himself as an advocate of taking people to their limits and, as an ardent people watcher, he makes the empirical link between stress and resilience and achievement. **Anthropologists now go further and say that without the evolution of the faculty for high stress levels we simply wouldn't be here at all!**

It is generally accepted that plant species lack the ability to fear and that is why they have evolved to a certain level and no further. They have proved perfectly capable of adapting to climate change and soil conditions but that's it. Trees, for instance, have never known how to worry, never experienced panic and, as a consequence, have never developed an ability to run away, let alone hide.

Birds, fishes and reptiles, governed by sophisticated reflex mechanisms in the brain, do, of course, know when they should flee. Mammals, on the other hand, also know *why* they should run from danger. Higher primates have evolved even further because of an ability to use fear to react in a uniquely creative manner to moments of danger and stress. And at the top of the order of apes, anthropologists now believe *Homo sapiens* reigned supreme, despite small teeth, no claws, comparatively little strength and a less than impressive running speed, by being just about the most frightened species on earth. More than any other animal we feared the elements and we learned to build rudimentary shelters, which in turn became fortifications; simple tools for foraging and cutting became weapons with which to defend and ultimately to attack.

So, primitive man survived because he constantly worried about predators and anxiously guarded the home, and became so scared that he had to do something about it! Those who knew no fear perished precisely because they took no precautions to ensure their survival. That's raw evolution. **And now we have evolved into a species that fears the wind and rain; the cold and the heat; thirst and hunger; heights and enclosed spaces; spiders and mice; dust and pollen and a thousand other enemies, but, perhaps above all others, The Four Stressers of the Apocalypse: Confusion, Embarrassment, Sarcasm and Discomfort. All of these can be used to ensure that your company gets the maximum performance from its 21st century anthropoids.**

STRESS POINT – Casual Atavism

Wait until a colleague is on their own and hurry into their office, throw your head back and feverishly sniff the air. Then climb on to their desk and squat in a primitive fashion before beginning a normal business-related conversation. If their phone rings, grunt and poke it before springing to the floor and running from the office.

STRESS AND CIVILIZATION

A long time after man had learnt to run and hide, huge empires were created, driven through fear of dominance by others and the strain of having to keep the populace fed and entertained. Emperors survived only by trusting no-one – and they perished if they did. Their people were kept in a constant state of anxiety, subjugated by leaders, threatened by barbarians and fearful of dominance by rival states. And, when times were really good, these empires diminished and fell. **There has never been a time in history when the complacent and the comfortable survived.**

Look at the ancient civilizations that are intrinsically linked to achievement and progress:

• **CHINA** – Home of porcelain and gunpowder, and yet, even as they studied the cosmos, the rulers of dynasties were forced to impose poetry, with all its wretched ability to unnerve and unsettle, upon a traditionally calm and contented people who, until then, had been planning to plant a hedge rather than build a wall.

• **EGYPT** – A land of arcane wisdom and extraordinary feats of civil engineering, and yet the hieroglyphs tell us that the inbred Pharaohs, themselves adorned in the most splendid garments, made loin cloths, with all the attendant embarrassments, mandatory for everyone in the knowledge that the vulnerable pick up slabs of stone more quickly.

• **GREECE** – A country of wine and philosophy, and yet, even with the discipline of a newly born logic, this legendary civilization was sustained by enforced role playing, the precursor of theatre, and the denial of alcohol to underachievers in their internecine wars, particularly those complacent visionaries responsible for the ill-fated three-man Trojan Squirrel.

• **ROME** – An empire of conquest and administration where intrigue energized the freshly bathed Caesars, who, as Pliny the Younger tells us, discovered that fickle loyalty could be consolidated by the ever-present opportunity to be personally introduced, in front of a crowd of strangers, to one of the larger and less convivial members of the cat family.

And all of these civilizations, like every other empire that has ever existed, crumbled or collapsed because their people – in particular the ruling elite – became comfortable and complacent and were replaced by the very people whom they had stimulated into action with fear and aspiration. The message is clear: The Stressed Shall Inherit the Earth!

In today's society, more people are stressed than ever before – not because of their intense lifestyles, but because evolution has gradually weeded out the casual and the less alert, has de-selected the apathetic and the nonchalant, and honed those better equipped to survive. Natural worriers have, over time, transmuted into stressful warriors. And it is precisely these survival traits which will determine the future of your company. **A thriving business, like an ancient empire, will only prosper as long as its ambitions and its aggression are matched by corresponding levels of stress. Captain Cook noted in his diary that, "*Stress is the handmaiden of discovery*", while Claudius said, "*Give me men who are anxious*". And Camus summed it up with, "*Only the dead don't worry.*"**

STRESS POINT – Verbal warnings to the undeserving

The people who need to be fully stressed up are the ones who have the most to offer – this can often be recognized because they are already making a greater contribution than their colleagues. So, do them a favour by acknowledging their ability to achieve. Begin a conversation with: "I've always been enormously disappointed with the quality of your work and wonder if you have a personal problem (obviously apart from your twitch), which you'd like to talk about. Anyway, regardless of circumstances, I'm putting you on warning that if things don't shape up buddy, I'm shipping you out!"

STRESS, THE MOTHER OF INVENTION

If we take a look at the major inventions of the last 500 years we will see that fear has continued to be the handmaiden of discovery throughout the centuries:

- 1440 – Johann Gutenburg, a religious chronicler, is threatened with expulsion from the church as no one, not even his mother, can understand his handwriting. Invents printing with movable type.

- 1590 – Cornelis Jansen, a Dutch watchmaker, develops a cleanliness fetish and vows to prove to sceptics and his long-suffering family that hands are covered in germs. Invents the microscope.

- **1608** – Hans Lippershey, a Dutch farmer, becomes obsessed with the fear that German mercenaries will enter the country to plunder his famous bulbs. Invents the telescope.

- **1643** – Evangelista Torricelli, an Italian mathematician, has a deranged wife who believes the devil gives her a headache every time she goes into the valley. Invents the barometer.

- **1714** – Gabriel Fahrenheit, a German physicist, fears his recent marriage will fail due to constantly arguing over the temperature in the bedroom. Invents mercury thermometer.

- **1752** – Benjamin Franklin fears the press will ignore him and, needing them to fulfil his political ambitions, seeks attention in a thunderstorm with a kite. Discovers lightning conductor.

- **1816** – Karl von Sauerbronn, a German cavalry officer develops an irrational fear of horses and is told by his commanding officer he will be courtmarshalled. Invents the bicycle.

- **1816** – Joseph Niepce, a famous beau in Paris, distrusts artists and is petrified that his rather startling good looks will be forgotten as time passes. Invents the camera.

- **1835** – Samuel Colt, the elderly owner of a confectioners in Dodge City, is taunted by school kids crowding his shop and stealing candy. Invents the revolving breech pistol.

- **1845** – Professor Anton von Schrotter, a newly appointed German philosopher, fears he will be unable to illustrate to his students the transience of our fragile lives. Invents the safety match.

- **1849** – Walter Hunt, an American office clerk, has an overriding fear that he will misplace pages from vital legal documents on his desk. Invents the safety pin.

- **1860** – Frederick Walton, a Manchester theatre owner, fears a tap dancer's metal heels will spark with nail heads on his wooden stage to cause a conflagration. Invents linoleum.

- **1866** – Alfred Nobel, a Swedish chemist, fears that noisy wedding guests in the newly built village hall next to his house will destroy his peace forever. Invents dynamite.

- **1867** – Lucien Smith, an experimental horticulturist from New Jersey, fears that vast flocks of passenger pigeons will alight on his hybrid maize crop. Invents barbed wire.

- **1884** – Lewis Waterman, oblivious to Burt's invention of the typewriter in 1829, fears an inability to write letters once birds have become extinct. Invents the fountain pen.

- **1887** – Adolf Fick, a German optician, fears that constant wearing of ubiquitous iron spectacles will eventually cause his nation to look northwards. Invents contact lenses.

- **1892** – Whitcomb Judson, a US manufacturer of sanitary-ware, fears that his newly introduced porcelain urinal will not catch on with a sceptical public. Invents the zip fastener.

- **1895** – King Camp Gillette, a clothier from Illinois, fears that the bobbles on his woollen sweaters caused by rough hands will deter customers. Invents the safety razor.

- **1900** – Horace Short, an early British spiritualist, fears that the newly deceased will be lost forever unless they clearly hear his directions on how to proceed. Invents the loudspeaker.

- **1900** – Johann Vaaler, a Norwegian towelling merchant, fears parents won't buy his newly marketed nappies unless they effectively stay on the baby. Invents the metal paper clip.

So, the answer to many of your company's problems, especially an inability to innovate or become market leaders, could be simply that your colleagues don't feel sufficiently threatened or frightened by rivals or colleagues. That will be simple to rectify when you let genuine stress empower them with a sense of commitment and urgency.

ANXIETY IS THE ROAD TO CREATIVITY

There isn't a genuine artist who doesn't know what it's like to suffer. And the bigger the misery, the harder they work. And the deeper the trough of despond, the more inspirational they become. And the further they fall into darkness, the more clearly and brilliantly their bruised hearts call out to the cold ear of an aching moon. Yes, true inventiveness comes at a price that is worth paying. **Identify the colleagues who will benefit from isolation and rejection and instil in them a sense of paranoia before giving them positions of authority where they can be a positive influence on the health of your company.**

THIRTEEN BEST STRESSED MEN

History is illuminated by beacons of stress who, in the Arts and Sciences, have towered over their talented but more relaxed contemporaries.

- **Plato** (circa 427BC–347BC)

- **Leonardo da Vinci** (1452–1519)

- **Nicolaus Copernicus** (1473–1543)

- **William Shakespeare** (1564–1616)

- **Galileo Galilei** (1564–1642)

- **Sir Isaac Newton** (1642–1727)

- **Wolfgang Amadeus Mozart** (1756–1791)

- **Ludwig van Beethoven** (1770–1827)

STRESS POINT – Hot Desking: space sharing to inconvenience the comfortable

This is a classic personnel initiative which invariably proves effective. Identify the happiest and most comfortable employee and ensure that, when they arrive for work one morning, there is at least one colleague now sharing their desk (note: maximum of three to a desk). This newcomer must already be highly stressed and, if possible, suffer from personal freshness problems, or, at the very least, be socially dysfunctional. The results of this quick and easy exercise need to be seen to be believed.

- **Louis Pasteur** (1822–1895)

- **Vincent Van Gogh** (1853–1890)

- **Sigmund Freud** (1856–1958)

- **Albert Einstein** (1879–1955)

- **Pablo Picasso** (1881–1973)

Chapter 2
The Health Argument

PROUD TO BE STRESSED!

Too many people, including employers, stigmatize stress as the new epidemic, an ailment, a weakness. This has resulted in work-related stress, according to a UK health and safety committee, being responsible for two-fifths of reported absenteeism. This is an astonishing 15 million work days lost because hard-working people have been made to feel that it is somehow wrong to display signs of stress to colleagues. Over half a million people, in the UK alone, have become ghettoized by this gross misinterpretation of a diagnosis and have chosen to stay at home.

Your colleagues must not, for obvious reasons, know that you have a strategy for creating and managing stress. It must never be acknowledged. They must, however, learn to accept stress as a badge of honour in others and, importantly, in themselves. **Companies, of course, have a duty to look after the physical and mental welfare of their employees and this naturally means encouraging those who are absent due to stress to return to work to proudly display the symptoms which uniquely qualify them to make an exceptional contribution to success.** A statement of courage always emboldens and inspires, and I recommend the mandatory wearing of badges bearing the legend, "Say Yes to Stress".

THE COMPLACENCY TRAP

It's not enough to encourage Stress Pride in order to persuade those who are off work to return. You will need to ensure that at least half the company is openly displaying signs of tension and anxiety coupled with job insecurity. **Don't allow contentment, let alone happiness, to creep its insidious way back into your company. If people are pleased with the job they have done it is your duty to disabuse them of their smugness. Satisfaction is the fast track to company malfunction.**

STIMULATION OF THE IMMUNE SYSTEM

A recent survey has shown that people displaying high levels of stress are less susceptible to acute ailments such as colds and flu. It's almost as though they're too busy to be caught by a bug but the reality is that adrenalin has ensured their immune system has all its fire walls up to offer extra protection to the body. **We can conclude that stressed people are much more healthy.**

THE ADRENAL GLAND AS COMPANY MOTIVATOR

We all know that in times of danger, fright, stress and anticipation, the two adrenal glands, ever-alert above each kidney and triggered by a signal from the autonomic nervous system, secrete the steroidal hormones adrenalin and noradrenalin. Now, let's remind ourselves of the truly exciting consequences:

- **The Bronchioles dilate** – More oxygen is made available for the production of energy.

- **Muscle of the gut relaxes** – Diaphragm lowers allowing increase in volume of air inhaled.

- **Glycogen in the liver converted to glucose** – Blood sugar level increases.

- **Heart rate and blood pressure increase** – Oxygen and glucose are distributed at a faster rate.

- **Blood diverted from reproductive systems** – More glucose and oxygen freed up for energy.

- **Digestion inhibited** – Blood diverted to muscles and other tissue involved in exertion.

- **Sensory perception increased** – More rapid reaction to external stimuli.

- **Mental awareness increased** – More rapid response to stimuli received.

- **Pupils in eyes dilated** – Range of vision increased.

- **Hair stands upright** – Gives threatened mammals the impression of increased size.

What we have above is a description of the perfect working beast – alert, excited, energized. Only three times have I been privileged to see hair standing completely upright. All were at moments of extreme challenge and commitment. The first occurred when a balding middle-aged manager was going for the ultimate sale, in order to save the company; the second was when a newly appointed young woman with shoulder-length blond hair was excitedly motivating her accounts team; the third happened during a role play where a heavily bearded castaway was standing barefoot on his desk when an over-zealous savage stuck a pencil in his ankle. Incredible!

STRESS AND SAFETY

Stress is not only an inhibitor of acute illnesses, it also ensures that workers are much less likely to suffer an industrial accident. Increased perception, wider range of vision and faster reactions, coupled with remarkable energy levels, ensure more alertness to potential dangers and a heightened ability to avoid them. **The stressed worker is a safe worker.**

AGITATION AS EXERCISE

People working under great pressure, which can often be self-imposed, benefit from regular secretions of high octane adrenalin, enabling them to maintain the optimum level of stress throughout the day. Pumped up and flying, these people can often display an almost startling level of enthusiasm and an astonishing work rate. **Reluctant and often unable to remain sedentary, they achieve a remarkable level of fitness while, at the same time, displaying a dynamism and sense of purpose, which quickly lead to achievement and status more relaxed, or moribund, colleagues will aspire to emulate.**

STRESS POINT – Office Switching

There are two methods of moving offices, both of which are highly effective in dramatically increasing stress levels:

• **Unannounced and unwelcome.** This depends on at least one of the participants being absent for a sufficient length of time to enable all their things to be moved to a smaller and poorly situated office. Experiment by not moving desks and chairs. It obviously helps if the other person involved in the exchange has less seniority.

• **Planned, unwelcome and weather-determined.** Both people involved are aware of the plan but have been informed that it is entirely dependent on the weather. For instance, "The move will begin within ten minutes of rain starting to fall," or, "You shall move when white fluffy clouds are gambolling like lambs across a blue meadow." This one can get interpretative but believe me it works.

CONTROLLING LUNCH BREAKS AS A MEANS TO WEIGHT LOSS

There is no doubt that the optimum adrenalin/body weight ratio is achieved by those individuals who weigh less than one would normally expect for their height and build. This allows adrenalin and its team-mate, noradrenalin, to kick-in earlier and with a more dramatic effect. By engendering a culture where lunch breaks are frowned upon (without of course putting anything in writing), it is a rewarding experience to witness how food deprivation, with naturally heavier individuals, can effect a dramatic weight loss accompanied by a commensurate increase in creative stress. With naturally slimmer people, lack of food quickly turns them into nervous, tense individuals who will soon realise their full potential.

Eating, just like drinking, is an habitual activity which is often used to regulate the pattern of the day rather than the nutritional needs of the body. If your colleagues prove to be dietary recidivists then it may be necessary to find a spurious reason to temporarily close the canteen or the kitchen. I have used plumbing and wiring as handy excuses to close dining areas, but late one evening I used a broom handle to effect a totally collapsed ceiling which took two weeks to fix, during which time productivity and creativity increased immeasurably (as did my bill at the dry cleaners).

ABSTINENCE AND EXCESS – THE TWIN PILLARS OF SUCCESS

It is all too easy to achieve the required level of stress and then let it gradually leach out of your company with sympathy or indulgence. Maintaining a hostile environment, where stress electrifies the corridors, is a challenge it would be wise to meet:

Ban all smoking, even in the smoking room. Tell these addicts that they can't go outside to puff because what is to stop someone else using that logic to have a sherbet break or a five minute whistle of their favourite tune. Where would the company be then?

Then, the next week, attempt to make smoking mandatory. Encourage abstainers to try smoking by buying them packets of cigarettes and then saying all smokers can have a 15 minute break every hour. Contrive passive smoking in meetings as much as possible so that stale, secondhand nicotine can enter virgin lungs and agitate and distress the recipients.

Then put a total ban on it once again and repeat the recipe in a few days time.

While doing this it makes sense to increase the general caffeine intake by introducing the twin dispensers of heightened awareness: espresso and cola machines. Offer them cheaper at first, like a dealer, to encourage experimentation, and then, when you've got them hooked, put the machines out of action for a few days.

STRESS POINT – Commando Speak: severing the normal lines of communication.

This strategy requires you to be alert at all times and to recognize the most strategically insensitive moment to interrupt an important conversation between two colleagues. Make sure you move swiftly to jump in between and tell the least startled of them that business has a lot to learn from the greatest film ever shown, The Ten Commandments, and that apart from the message it still makes you cry.

A similar manoeuvre can be used in hand-to-hand conversation in a corridor. Stare intently into the eyes of the speaker and look out for the most inappropriate mid-sentence moment to interrupt. Shout "DOWN" and knock them to the floor, leaping on top in a protective manner. Get up and check the wall for bullet holes. Re-start the conversation with "Sorry, you were saying?"

Put all of it together and you'll be standing in the Temple of Stress. I have heard of a 35% increase in productivity from one company who adopted this regime. Thus, denial of food, caffeine and nicotine can help to create the ultimate competitive working environment.

STOPPING THE RIGHT SIDE OF TRAUMA

Everyone is a different shaped vessel into which stress can be poured and it makes sense, as far as is practicable, to establish individual needs and capacities. The simplest way to do this is to create a stress monitor spreadsheet on which you can plot the progress of an individual or a department. Observe what is accepted as normal and then, using the methods described in this book, proceed to immerse your colleague in a stressful environment. For some, a gradual approach is easier to control, but you will no doubt identify other members of the team who will benefit from a huge intake of pure stress, like a bolt of lightning, which will immediately transform them into intellectual powerhouses with an almost superhuman capacity for work. You may observe from a distance that raw fear in action has an almost primordial beauty.

However, there are others, small in number but nevertheless widespread, who are evolutionary throwbacks to ancestral casualness. No matter how much they are cajoled, coerced, duped or threatened, they respond with an insouciance that explains why they are a dying breed. There are actually two types of these characters: the first seem impervious to stress, which runs off them like water, while the second are incapable of keeping it and are laughing again within five minutes. It's as though they were colanders through which anxiety quickly drains away. These would be the people incapable of building shelters, reluctant to turn ploughshares into swords and who would stand with a tray of herbal teas and organic flapjacks as the Mongol Hordes rode into town. The Stressed shall leave them behind as surely as Neanderthal Man failed to follow us into civilization.

However, though the future most certainly is Stress, it must be acknowledged that there are others who, through no fault of their own, find pressure sufficiently disturbing as to detach them from normal patterns of behaviour. Even small quantities can give them an emotional shock and temporarily unhinge them, and deep draughts of stress, voluntarily consumed, can actually permanently traumatize. It is absolutely vital for the effective running of your company that you learn to identify such individuals so that you don't hire them in the first place. If you are unfortunate enough to inherit them, on the other hand, you must keep them outside the normal rules of engagement until you have an opportunity to gently dispense with their services for the sake of your company's health.

Learn how to unsettle the mind without causing permanent derangement. Use the Stress Chart to stop in time.

Apart from the above there are very few negative consequences to the introduction of a stressful environment. I have actually come across only one example in a long career where an individual (for whom as it turned out, any level of stress was entirely inappropriate) was subjected to a high degree of pressure and reacted in an unpredictable fashion. I'm afraid she leapt the entire trauma stage. Within five minutes of me telling her that her report was worthless (it was actually excellent) and needed to be completely re-written that evening, she had kicked me on the shin, held a brass paperknife to my throat and, with a typical feat of psychopathic strength, had beaten me about the head with my own laptop.

STRESS POINT – Senseless acts of random madness

Spill your drink on someone eminently decent who is about to conclude the conversation by making an excellent and valid point. I've found it equally effective in meetings or on a one-to-one basis in the corridor – but I learned to pay attention to the temperature of the liquid when I discovered burns units are unpleasant places to visit and are often inconveniently situated out of town.

A great variation (best with water in a plastic cup) is to throw the lot over the groin area of a colleague wearing a expensive and fashionable light-coloured suit.

Chapter 3
The Business Imperative

STRESSED TO KILL

There is no doubt that we are entering a sustained period of uncertainty in domestic economies and violent swings in the global market, and many weaker companies will either collapse or be taken by predators. This is nothing to do with size but everything to do with culture and attitude. Stress will be the key to success. The behaviour of a business, whether it be a workshop or an international conglomerate, should reflect the instincts of primitive man. Trust in nothing. Hide when you have to and fight when you can. If there's a beast in the forest, make sure it finds some easier prey than you. Work with those you can trust but don't trust too much. Take more than you give. **And remember, it's not the one who doesn't blink, it's the one who stays awake.**

You've earned a reputation for reliability so keep it. Co-operation is the cornerstone of reassurance for both suppliers and customers and you need both of them to trust you in the forest. Thus, build your shelter, run from the rain, but be strong enough to help others whom you may need in the future. Make sure that every member of your company carries as much stress as they can healthily bear. Each of them must manifest the attributes of your business.

Don't forget your two Colt 45s, adrenalin and noradrenalin, and keep them shooting all the time. Respect danger and fear it, anticipate conflict and feel the stress levels soar exultantly. We could be talking about an internal meeting or a clash with one of the big boys. It doesn't matter. Providing you and your colleagues are stressed to the hilt you'll represent a formidable challenge to anyone and anything. Remember the advantages you have: extra oxygen and increased blood sugar levels for superior energy and genuine staying power; a faster reaction to external stimuli and increased mental awareness; an increased range of vision so that every muscle twitch is perceived. And maybe, just maybe, there will come that special moment when you feel your hair suddenly and magnificently rise to the occasion.

THE FIVE FACES OF STRESS

Once you have sought out and destroyed every innate tendency to complacency and enjoyment within your company, you will feel a stimulating and almost palpable change in the environment. When you are used to working in these liberating conditions and are fully confident in your ability to increase pressure and discomfort as and when required, you will begin to recognize the different types of stress that manifest themselves. Everyone's stress, like a fingerprint, is unique, with its own pattern of behaviour, but for practical purposes I tend to place the different types within five distinct families:

STRESS TYPES

- **Negative stress** – Manifestation: unproductive illness – Action: write to the employee explaining that he/she should be proud to be stressed and encourage them to return to work to set an example to colleagues. Remember to enclose their "Say Yes to Stress" badge.

- **Defensive stress** – Manifestation: a debilitating tendency to mistrust motives – Action: give them the means to increase the stress levels of colleagues.

- **Aggressive stress** – Manifestation: inaccurate targeting and misdirected energy – Action: use their rage to help immediate colleagues and against those whom you'd like to resign.

- **Creative stress** – Manifestation: ideas and limbs flying in all directions coupled with an awesome inability to relax – Action: up the caffeine input and step back.

- **Competitive stress** – Manifestation: the truly wonderful sight of a manic, high speed, totally alert and empowered individual, incapable of leaving his post, skin taut on his gaunt face and red and staring eyes. He can see into the minds of others and climb the outside of buildings – Action: none required.

Once you have identified the different stress types you can assess their abilities along with the requirements of your business. Place them on your Stress Chart and put the two together. This will assist you in determining the types of individuals you may need to recruit should some of your present colleagues fail to reach acceptable levels of stress.

RECRUITMENT

Remember when interviewing that you should be tough with candidates and put them under considerable pressure. Those who withstand your onslaught of sarcasm, ridicule, intrusive questioning and studied bad manners will identify themselves as unsuitable to join your company. But be constantly aware that they may be near to breaking point and so you should try a little harder to increase the tension. Remember that it's not enough to be vulnerable and feeble-minded, and some of the more cerebral but stoic characters may eventually break under questioning and prove themselves to be the highly intelligent nervous wrecks that you are looking for.

TRAINING

Don't waste a valuable training budget by spending it on your staff, let alone on an entire woodland survival course or a paint ball yard, or a whitewater experience coupled with hugging a cliff face with their groins. **The biggest need your business will ever have is for more top quality anxiety and pressure. This book can be read as a training manual for stress.**

If you really do feel the need to get formal with your stress training then make sure it costs very little and is not in business time. For instance, I once told my entire company that they'd earned a reward for hitting target and I'd organized a big surprise for the weekend. I arranged to meet them outside the office at 7.30am on Saturday and they all turned up looking very excited with their overnight bags, cameras and showing one another their passport photos. I walked them to the local park where I lined them up and divided them into Cowboys and Indians. I made the most pathetic individual in both teams either the Indian chief or the cavalry captain and told them they all had ten minutes to find good sticks. Meanwhile I lined up their luggage like the crenellations of a fort. When they returned with their weapons I made them whoop and shoot and die in public, ensuring the final massacre took place on a football pitch where two under-9s teams were being watched by their proud parents. Later that day, I told my staff in Accident & Emergency (or at least the ones like me who'd had only local anaesthetics) that I had noted how most of them had grown in stature as the morning progressed.

Chapter 4
Trojan Horses

However successful your campaign to deride and rule, there will still be massive and exciting opportunities to undermine the confidence of the entire company and to create wall-to-wall stress. These opportunities must be taken to ensure that your company retains a competitive advantage. Look at your diary for the year and, if there are not regular opportunities for all employees, or at least complete departments or teams, to be gathered together, then quickly do something about it or you may never witness that exquisite moment of mass confusion which ripples into distress and blind panic. The high level stress is almost palpable. It travels like a contagion and infects and energizes even the most robust and relaxed individuals and will have a long-lasting effect on the morale of your company.

CALENDAR ENGINEERING

Always start with the assumption that there is very little in your diary that cannot be moved with impunity (apart, as I've learnt to my cost over the years, the funerals of colleagues). Appointments with customers, clients and the media must of course be treated with a healthy respect born of the knowledge that their magic can be harmful or elevating. However, your relationships with colleagues will benefit from cancelling meetings at the last minute or, more imaginatively, moving them to improbable times or implausible locations. Mix both and see an effervescence, which fizzes into a creativity that can last for weeks before starting to go flat. And then you can repeat the dosage.

Several years ago I worked briefly as a consultant for a leading environmental charity, which, although large and successful, was far too pleased with itself, and many of its employees had become enervated and smug. I arranged for 20 fundraisers from all over the country to meet in a café in Smithfield Market at 7.00am one Monday morning in January. I felt, quite rightly as it turned out, that some of them would be stimulated by so many men in white coats covered in blood. I ensured that their manager, who picked me up from home, arrived late by directing him the scenic route. I told him to park outside, sound his horn and stride in, which he did, and the meeting was a complete success. It included several arguments between charity workers and regulars who couldn't find a seat, didn't want to listen to the speeches and whose heckling, although unimaginative, was loud and to the point.

The young manager himself was completely frayed by 9 o'clock, an added benefit I had anticipated, and, long after his team had evacuated the café, he continued to ask me, somewhat emotionally, about motivation and leadership. I wondered if he was capable of driving home but found this was of academic concern as his Fiat estate had four perfectly flat tyres, courtesy of a fundraiser from Eastbourne, who had carefully written *with love from Davinia* in lipstick on his nearside window. I concluded that this must have been before the bright yellow wheel clamp had been added, like irony, to the offside front wheel. His hands trembled in the freezing rain as he peeled the giant sticker from the windscreen and I had to point out to him that a forklift truck had pronged his back window. The gist of the unsigned post-it note from the absent truck driver was that it was less than sensible to park near a corner and we could keep the sheep carcass, in repose amongst the shattered glass in the back of the car, as it should have been incinerated a week ago.

The effect was extraordinary: as I witnessed bolts of stress shake him to the core, I knew that his performance levels would reach undreamed-of heights and that he would be changed forever. I can't claim the credit for orchestrating the entire proceedings, but I

STRESS POINT – Nil-by-mouth: signalling your intentions

Institute Semaphore Tuesday when only movements of the head, hand signals and small sandcastle flags can be used for internal communication including, of course, meetings. Let it be known that talkers and other transgressors will be disciplined. In the short term a more sophisticated form of body language will evolve, which, over the weeks, will develop into lithe elitism from some and seething resentment from others with less articulate bodies. The ensuing chaos will result in most workers ceasing to communicate on Tuesdays. Expect solo performances of frenetic and productive activity. You can confuse the smug by raising your left knee, smacking it once with your right hand and then, swaying from side to side, opening and closing your mouth like a fish.

humbly suggest that it seems God sometimes enters the business world to help an individual achieve his full potential. Although in this case it certainly wasn't me, as the cheque the charity sent got lost in the post and I eventually tired of threatening them with legal action.

ROLLING METAMORPHOSES

One of the most effective methods of galvanising your company is to arrange a staff picnic. Best, of course, is a Saturday in either Spring or Autumn so that there can be genuine apprehension about the weather. Don't spend a lot of money by taking them somewhere pleasant but hire cheap coaches (*Charabanc* written on the sides is a good sign) and take them to the nearest grim seaside spot. Remember that being downwind of a nuclear power station always helps hypochondriacs to avoid relaxing. Wait until they've settled on the beach and the brave have put on their costumes, and then stand on someone else's wicker picnic basket and ask them all to gather round as you have something to say. Thank them for coming and tell them you hope there will be time for games after you've all eaten, but first you want to go through the latest company results. Apologize that you're going to go into detail, but tell them that it's important they get a proper sense of where the company is at the moment. Sufficiently important, in fact, that there will be a small quiz emailed on Monday. But not to worry because anyone scoring under 20 points will join the Monday Morons for a training session that evening which can be extended to include memory skills.

Once you have finished your speech you must invite team leaders to each spend ten minutes updating the company on their progress. When the last has finished speaking, call them all up around the picnic basket and say, "Before we applaud, I just want to say that without exception, those were the most inane and unappealing speeches ever to pollute this beach. Churchill would have left you dead in the sand." Then clap.

Get more upbeat and announce that, quite obviously, team leader roles need to be reviewed next week but, meanwhile, let's not forget that each of these people is not a total failure and that they have, in the past, performed well for the company. However, we now have to move forwards.

What I've described is the great business jive – genuine big roll metamorphoses which can effortlessly turn a staff picnic into an outdoor company meeting into a killing field into a garden of remembrance.

THE SALES CONFERENCE AS A GATHERING OF THE FALLEN

So many companies make the mistake of building a sense of excitement for a forthcoming conference, which culminates in an orchestrated event of unparalleled boredom where ennui ripples like corrugation down the faces of the living dead as deep veined thrombosis rises from their feet.

Yes, conferences must be keenly anticipated but with the same sharp expectancy that Edward II had for the poker heating in the fire. Use a very different technique to that which you would employ for a company picnic. Planning is everything. Insist that plans are made much earlier than usual, including detail, and then have weekly meetings at which you systematically change them. Follow the stress trail from demoralization to demotion and choose the action least likely to damage the performance of your company prior to the conference and most likely to unsettle the actual event. Remember, memorial services can galvanize a people. But never forget that memorial services require victims. **So, the business message is clear, slaughter a few egos before the ceremony and, just to keep things lively, let it be known that there is at least one unsuspecting goat still being fattened.**

STRESS POINT – Hot Wiring

Wait until a colleague has temporarily left their office and quickly nip in and send a salacious or otherwise inappropriate email to a vulnerable or dangerous colleague. Repeat this exercise regularly until you achieve a result.

Two well-tried alternatives are to use the same computer to send filthy and childish memos to half the company or to identify one person who would benefit from receiving similar correspondence from a number of unwitting colleagues. The last can be enormously effective in reducing torpor in the recipient but is much more difficult to achieve as it requires a combination of access to offices and secrecy. Still, in my experience, it's always worth a try.

THE CHRISTMAS PARTY AS
THE HALL OF SACRIFICE

This festive gathering is normally the last opportunity of the year to engender widespread stress and is the perfect venue for ensuring that your staff go into the holiday period in the right frame of mind so that they will return to work devoid of indolence and apathy.

Here's how you do it: make it fancy dress. It's always easier to humiliate someone if unmasking can be part of the process. Take the microphone before the band starts and announce that there will be a competition to see who looks the biggest idiot in their costume. That will unnerve everyone and make your next statement more potent. Say no, but seriously, there will be a competition to decide who has been the least effective member of the company in the last year. First, though, let's all enjoy our complimentary drink as we listen to the band.

When the band have finished the first part of their gig, take the stage clapping enthusiastically and thank them, adding that they'll need to play a couple of dirges after the break as the competition winners are just about to be announced. Announce third position and get them up on to the stage as their colleagues applaud. List their faults and inadequacies, hand over a box of chocolates, shake hands or air kiss and, just as they leave, however clever or obvious their costume, ask them who they are supposed to be.

Treat second place in a similar fashion but be harsher as they have performed to an even lower standard for your company. Give them a smaller box of chocolates. Ridicule the costume and ask them to take their mask off if they're not wearing one.

Now first place is different. This is a person you decided some time ago has no place in your organization, but you have waited until this moment to go public as it will have the most positive effect on their colleagues. Say the prize is for sloth, inadequacy, carelessness and kibosh, and this year you are delighted that there is a unanimous winner of the SICK award. It goes to someone whom all will agree has wildly exceeded the rigorous criteria for first prize. Ladies and Gentleman, it's my pleasure to announce... But, take note: be merciful when they come on stage. Shake hands and quickly hand them their dismissal letter, whisper that you've checked and it's legal, and then clap them off before announcing that here come the band so let's all take to the floor and boogie. **Be confident that this dismissal is necessary, and that there will be huge benefits for the rest of the team, who will now remain fully stressed through a period which is traditionally associated with relaxation.**

THE CONSULTANT AS ASSASSIN

We all know that the Assassins originated in 11th century Persia as a fearsome and mysterious sect famed for their ability to seek out their target and eliminate them. I have always seen this as the main role of a consultant who, called in to identify a problem and then to eliminate it, behaves precisely as a modern day Assassin – particularly as the difficulty is invariably one of personnel.

It's vital that your staff believe from the start that the consultant has come in to recommend job cuts. I mean, they won't really believe it but it's a collective indulgence perpetrated by any group of people who actually believe they are safe. The consultant will come in and the stress levels will rise. It's as simple as that. No need for tough talking, all he or she has to do is walk around and look sinister. You will already know those who have slipped back toward relaxation and the consultant can, particularly on Semaphore Tuesday, by a little nuance of behaviour, perhaps the blade of the hand moving quickly across the throat, clearly indicate to them that they are vulnerable.

Don't underestimate the powers of perception held by the consultant. As soon as he arrives on his first day you will get your money's worth just by asking him to spend a quarter of an hour walking around the office space. Then ask him who his instinct tells him is superfluous to requirements, immediately call this person into your office and dismiss them. It's as easy as that. Whatever the consultant later recommends, however far-reaching the proposals, nothing will beneficially affect the corporate stress levels as much as the action taken on that first morning. **Remember that every assassination is protecting someone else and, in the case of your company, saving jobs.**

> ## STRESS POINT – Negative Encouragement: laughter is the best medicine
> There are occasions when, confronted by a brilliant idea or offered an eminently sensible recommendation, there is simply no other response than, "Ha ha ha, that's a good one!" This undermines someone who is quite probably an excellent worker already and will help take them to new levels of achievement.

MISPLACED KINDNESS AS A WEAPON OF MASS DESTRUCTION

It is all too easy for a manager to be gratuitously unpleasant or obsequiously nice, but a thoughtful strategy brings a mixture of the two approaches so that there can be an unsettling inconsistency to the management of people. I remember I once spent several months roundly complimenting an elderly finance director and his three managers – all of whom inspired absolutely no confidence at all. Their huge department was the scene of an almost brutal, yet casual, incompetence and I was aware that the situation could not go on. At the end of the financial year their crimes against monetary laws were quickly discovered by the auditors, the dogs of wealth, who tore into our books with a ferocity that demanded that the team at the top of accounts left the same week. **In business, there is nothing wrong with the Judas kiss providing tongues are not involved.**

Chapter 5
Mussolini's Revenge

Mussolini said, *"Those who are habitually late are time delinquents, thieves, criminals who take moments and sometimes hours from others and yet because of their weakness are unable ever to see the complete picture themselves."* So, poor time-keeping has been recognized for some time as a crime against society and we have all learned that it is not too difficult to deal with recidivists by threatening them with disciplinary action if they re-offend. But the vast majority of workers do consistently arrive when they should and it's a much greater challenge to deal in an effective and stressful manner with good time-keepers. One method I've used myself is to constantly, almost from week to week, change the hours of work. At the very least this causes confusion and breaks up the commuter's regular timetable, not allowing them to settle or relax. If your day ends at 5.30 on Friday then wait until 5.25 before announcing by email that working hours have changed for the following Monday. If this meets with dissent, so much the better. Tell them that if they don't like the system you will draw start times out of a hat at lunchtime every day.

PUBLIC TRANSPORT – THE WHEELS OF MISFORTUNE
Once you have begun to change working hours on an irregular basis

you can capitalize on the uncertainty and disruption this causes in even the most reliable of colleagues. Every time someone is late for work – a good yardstick is more than three minutes – ask them to fill in a public transport register which names the route and the personal name and number of the bus, tram or train driver who has transgressed. That lunchtime your late colleague must have pursued their complaint with the transport company and reported the reasons for delay in the register. There will inevitably be a conscientious and valuable member of staff who will be unfortunate enough to travel on a route which is notoriously poorly served by public transport. This presents you with an ideal opportunity to make an example of them. Tell them that if they are late two days in a row you will be obliged to begin disciplinary proceedings which quite possibly will result in termination of employment. For the benefit of all those struggling with the vicissitudes of public transport put the following on the notice board: BETTER NEVER THAN LATE!

REGIMENTALIZATION – THE ROUTE MARCH TO INSTABILITY

Corridors are like roads and workers must walk on the same side as cars. I don't believe this for a minute but sign this edict and put it up on the notice board and you'll see some interesting results as the majority quickly conform and a few free spirits challenge your authority as they swerve from side to side. I recommended this policy to a friend, Mike, after I told him his import business, which had been running for several years, felt more like a friendly village than a commercial concern. Productivity measurably increased as he took it further and painted no stopping lines along walkways and placed cones around offices where he wanted people not to be disturbed. I guess he took it close to its limit when he got his 14-year-old daughter to come in on her holidays to take Polaroids of people walking on the wrong side of the corridor. Mike's business had peaked and I firmly believe it wouldn't have lasted anyway, but he erroneously blames me for the suggestion that his daughter stick parking tickets on the backs of those who stopped to chat. Apparently that move coincided with it all beginning to fall apart for Mike. Not long after, both business and marriage seemed to hold hands and dive together into the abyss.

Here's another good one to try: we all know that there is an ergonomically correct way of picking up the phone, I recommend you insist this is made best practice within your organization. When listening, there is a proper position for the earpiece which causes least damage to the tympanum: tell staff that there will be spot checks when the switchboard alerts security that phones are in use. Instruct your staff that they must all use the same greeting, for instance, "Good morning, my name is Rita, how may I help you? Calls may be monitored for training and security purposes..." even when they know it's an internal call.

I once did consultancy for a linen company and introduced them to the Ecolec Line Break, a system sadly demised (as indeed are my clients) but much lamented by those of us who can recall how knowing the electronic timer would cut off the call after exactly five minutes concentrated minds wonderfully. However, I find the most effective method of regulation is Coin Box Conversing. Install a wall-mounted payphone in every office, and give each employee coins to cover their conversations for the week. Ensure the amount is woefully inadequate, so that stress levels can be matched by cost-cutting.

STRESS POINT – Groom at the top

In a meeting wait until someone is in full flow and lean across to brush both of their shoulders with your hand. Do it carefully and then peer at your handiwork before returning to the left shoulder and flicking an imaginary larger flake of dandruff into the ether. This exercise, simple but effective in reducing calm, can be even more effective when you next see the person in the corridor, and can be coupled with a quick glance at each of their shoes.

Repeat as necessary.

THE BEAUTY OF ORDER

If the company culture has an air of fragility then it's an easy step to use it as a metaphor for what must be achieved on a personal basis by each of your colleagues if they are to give you their maximum output. If you've looked at time-keeping and corridor etiquette you should now turn your attention to areas where a firm insistence on a policy of cleanliness and neatness will bring a commensurate increase in anxiety and self-inflicted pressure. Don't be over-ambitious. Divide your office space into areas: i.e. personal offices; general offices; copying rooms; meeting rooms; kitchen/canteen. Select one of them and then list the items which would benefit from being lined up or stacked in a way that suggests a controlled and minimalist environment. Fully implement your plan for this area before beginning the next.

Choose a sensitive colleague and, in their absence, pile up all the loose papers on their desk and make a bundle of their pens with a rubber band. Put everything you find on the floor, including files, in a stack under their desk, or, depending on the effect you think it will have, on their chair. Then spray strong disinfectant on their keyboard and the mouthpiece of the phone as well as the door handle as you leave. And possibly a flourish around their seat if it's not covered in detritus from the floor.

This simple yet helpful gesture will result, if my experience is anything to go by, in a colleague so taut and focused that the energy exuded can briefly externalize into an open physical attack on the innocent. It is important that no one must know you were involved. Timing is everything and you must give yourself plenty of time to make yourself scarce.

The first occasion on which I experimented with this strategy was in the office of a particularly strident commercial director. She reacted poorly to the discovery that a contract waiting for signature was damp and, so she claimed, that the room smelt like a newly cleaned toilet. I escaped serious injury only by hiding on the metal fire escape. I remember the door closed behind me, and, when darkness fell, I made my way in the sleet down the metal stairs to the empty car park. Reception was locked. I was in my shirtsleeves and my jacket and coat, along with my wallet and car keys, were inside the building. I expected an ambush at any moment from this incandescent colleague as I set off down the winding unlit lane to the main road. It took three hours to walk the ten miles home, by which time I was suffering from mild frostbite and my jaws ached from shivering, but I fondly remember the warm glow induced by the knowledge that I had taken my protagonist to such an intensity of stress that the entire company would benefit from my altruism.

Whether it's chairs in telesales, documents on a desk, notices on a pinboard, cups in a kitchen or coasters in a meeting room, everyone will benefit if they are forced to maintain strict geometric lines and patterns. This will, of course, disregard personal preferences so that, for instance, all revolving chairs will have to be set at the same height. If they don't do it, they lose it. It's as simple as that. **But make sure you're not over-ambitious. My strong advice is start with an individual and a small working space and then gradually expand. Remember, Rome wasn't destroyed in a day.**

STRESS POINT – Gender Discomfort

I'm afraid that the days when lewd suggestions and salacious remarks could embarrass and demoralize are long gone and, in a more sophisticated environment, you may need to pursue gender stress into the toilet. Without prior consultation, remove the male/female signs from the doors and announce by an email (the word even suggests an hermaphrodite), headed "Evacuation Procedures", that all toilets are mixed sex with immediate effect and that it would be discriminatory for people to continue their cloakroom apartheid. Set an example by choosing the toilet which had recently been for the opposite sex and, when you're in a cubicle, strike up a conversation as soon as you hear footsteps. Alternatively, when you're at the washbasins and mirrors, ask the unknown person behind the closed door what their favourite sound is. Try to keep the conversation relevant without becoming crass.

PUNISHING THE INNOCENT

You can be confident that, properly maintained, your regime of order and self-discipline will take your company stress levels to a height which should give you a tangible competitive advantage over businesses deluded into thinking an enlightened culture will bring them success. However, even before the new order was imposed, you would have had members of staff who, in terms of speed, accuracy, neatness and timekeeping, were such paragons of misplaced virtue that, by their very acts of efficiency, they induced stress – at times bordering on genuine nausea – in more lethargic colleagues.

There is a danger that the original tidiness/cleanliness fetishists within your company will see their policy of order and disinfectant, once ridiculed by their colleagues, as now entirely vindicated and could, in my experience, believe they have arrived in the promised land. I recall one particular manager who, after I had created his longed-for Euclidean world of angles and lines, began to see himself as a prophet and took to wandering among his distressed and overwrought colleagues, dispensing rather unoriginal homilies on cleanliness and godliness. Unfortunately, the increased unpopularity this brought him, rather than inducing evangelical paranoia and unhappiness, encouraged him to take on the calm and stoic demeanour of a persecuted holy man. In fact his calmness became palpable and unbearable, and I remember the appalling afternoon when he was hounded by colleagues in the corridor and sought refuge in my office. This was bad enough but his wild eyes then began to stare at my rather busy looking desk. He reached out his hands and I thought he was granting me absolution, but instead he began to reassemble the report I had carefully separated and to neatly rebuild my post-it-note pad with numerous notes I had stuck around my phone. I got up just as the yellow duster was emerging from his trouser pocket and, without a word, I opened the door in the hope that the mob would come in and lynch him. Alas, they had been dispersed by a work experience line monitor called Heather, who, I'm proud to say, now runs a private prison in Yorkshire.

So, what can be done to these people who, though they may always suffer from residual self-righteousness, can still be rescued and re-introduced to a life of anxiety? Plenty! I don't need to go into detail but I want to.

Their office or work space, a shining beacon of order, must be gradually brought down to scratch. Find a tube of handcream in a female colleague's top drawer and, after liberally applying it to your own hard-working hands, go to the screen of the cleanliness freak who is suffering from calm. This is, of course, best done in the evening so that no one sees you wiping your hands all over the computer screen and so the creative smears (you can do pictures if you want) will have dried by the morning.

Choose additional options from the following list to ensure the rescue is a complete success. Implement them all at the same time and witness a magnificent surge on the national stress grid.

QUICK AND EASY PRACTICAL TIPS FOR SAVING THE RIGHTEOUS

- **Chewing gum under desk**

- **Coffee splashes on ceiling**

- Collection of clients' business cards replaced with more colourful ones from a public phone box.

- Dubious streaks on floor

- Favourite mug left on desk, smelling of disinfectant, with the attached note saying "Thanks. Got the all clear!"

- Lentil soup, with carrot and sweetcorn, in waste basket

- Mucus on keyboard

- Muddy footprints on cabinet

- Pencil shavings ground into carpet

- Re-arranged filing system

- Small chunks of cheese on mousemat

- Splashed milk on chair

- Tiny pieces of food on phone mouthpiece

- Unpeelable sticker on window

Warning: don't tamper with electrics unless you really know what you're doing.

CHAPTER 6
NEW AGE TYRANNY

In a new age of uncertainty, when people can change beliefs as often as clothes, you mustn't underestimate the power of ideas which were once considered unorthodox but are now in general currency amongst the weak and the vulnerable. The ability to unsettle at will is obviously desirable and the techniques required should be carefully selected according to whether you wish to cause general panic and mass hysteria or individual terror and private anguish.

It can normally take up to eight weeks for a new member of staff to become fully acclimatized and to relinquish their previous personae sufficiently to enable them to adapt to the group culture of their new place of work. Two months of working on less than maximum output is simply unacceptable for a commercial operation and you must plan to acclimatize a new recruit within, wherever possible, the first day. You believe they are susceptible to stress, otherwise you wouldn't have hired them. At the interview you must have caused genuine tension or at the very least sensed that it would be possible to create within them great anxiety. So, work quickly before they come under the influence of their new colleagues. You want a situation where they are deeply uncomfortable (at the very least!) with what they have witnessed or endured, but find themselves in a position where they have no one with whom they can share the burden. **Bottled-up, 90% proof stress** is the nearest thing to an internal explosion that most people could have the privilege of experiencing. However, always remember to stop just the right side of trauma.

SPONTANEOUS COMBUSTION

This one has never failed me and requires very little preparation or materials for impressive results, but, like many of the individual techniques, it ideally requires the victim in question to remain silent about their ordeal. You need:

- **One household candle**

- **One incense stick plus holder**

- **One box of matches**

- **One pot of ash**

- **One decorative cushion**

- **One small vase of cheap flowers**

You must obtain a decent amount of ash and bring it to work in a small jar with a screw top. Any grey and finely powdered sort will do but ash from a woodland bonfire is, apart from High Grade Crematorium, probably the best you can have.

Before they arrive on their first day you must burn some cheap sandalwood incense in their office and while doing so stand on their chair, light the candle, and blacken the patch of ceiling above it with smoke, taking care not to ignite the building.

Then sprinkle one handful of ash on the chair and gently blow it towards the crease where the seat meets the back. Fabric is always best for this sort of thing, so institute a company policy of not buying leather or plastic chairs. Push the ash into the crease with your fingers so that it could appear that a half-hearted attempt has been made by a bored cleaner to vacuum it up.

Put a smaller amount of ash on your hand and blow some into the shelves and amongst the files so that it can be discovered. A tiny amount filtered into the keyboard is also recommended.

Relight the candle and carefully burn two large oval holes, next to one another and facing the desk, in the seat of the chair. Make sure that nothing is still alight when you place the decorative cushion on top.

Put the vase of flowers on the window ledge, pick up the incense holder and leave the room, closing the door behind you to retain the smell of burning but ostensibly to engender a sense of privacy so that the newcomer will feel like an intruder.

When the new recruit arrives take them straight from reception to their office. Apologise that you have a meeting and tell them the best possible way they can spend the day is to look at the reports you've left on their desk. Just as you're leaving say, "Oh, just one more thing. I'm afraid we've got some rather sensitive little souls here who claim that the room still smells of burning and like the door to be kept shut so they don't get upset. Pathetic isn't it? It was obviously tragic the way we lost both of them like that. Extraordinary I suppose you could say. Two within six months. And yet I don't completely buy this idea of spontaneous combustion, do you? But what a coincidence, eh?"

STRESS POINT – Title Confusion

Positions and titles are hugely important to the over-inflated and the insignificant and you must take full advantage of these status-conscious colleagues by changing their appellation whenever it seems inappropriate. These should be announced by email and rescinded by rumour – and sometimes vice versa – and there should be a genuine sense of injustice about the whole procedure. The monthly updated phone list is an opportunity not only to change titles en masse but also, as a consequence, to dramatically change the lines of reporting. Those who you think will be particularly distressed by this simple move should also have their names misspelled.

ALIEN ABDUCTION

This is more ambitious than spontaneous combustion but has the advantage that it can be done at any time. All it requires is three very small circular holes to be burnt in the centre of the chair before you place the ubiquitous cushion on top. Tell the newcomer how reassured you are that at last you have a sane and robust person in the position. Explain how sensitive the rest of the staff are and so no one must ever know what you are about to tell. Say you don't believe it for a minute but just in case there is any truth in what you were told by the three previous incumbents in the job, you feel you must now tell what each of them said in confidence before they left.

None of them, as far as you know, had ever met, and yet, within three months of joining, each of them had mysteriously disappeared for several hours before re-appearing in their office, perched rather uncomfortably on their chairs, and telling almost identical stories. Their eyes were startled, their clothing was undone and dishevelled and they had spoken with strangely high voices. Each had been sitting working on their computer when the screen had gone dead for several seconds before it glowed ultra-violet and the words appeared, in a colour unknown to man, "YOU DWELL IN THE PORTAL OF GHAN." Each of them then claimed that they lost the power of speech as they felt themselves pulled, as one of them put it, away from themselves. They reappeared naked in a white, circular room on a spaceship. A young woman, shining like purple neon and holding a miniature light sabre, transmitted her words into their heads and said, "I AM THE KEEPER OF THE PORTAL OF GHAN AND YOU SHALL STAND AT MY SIDE AS SENTINEL AND SHALL CARRY INSIDE YOU THIS BURNING SPEAR OF DESTINY." They couldn't move as she floated towards them and then each of them had broken down and couldn't finish their story. In fact, each of them, over that dreadful ten months, had sobbed uncontrollably and then hobbled out of the office forever.

DIVINE INTERVENTION AND DIVINE RETRIBUTION

These two are closely allied and no preparation is required in order to convince members of staff that God, moving in His mysterious ways, has decided to take an interest in the company.

Call a staff meeting and, standing on a chair, put your hands in the air to announce that The Lord spoke to you just half an hour ago in the lift and said, "To those who toil shall come reward, to those who idle shall come justice." Explain that it's obviously good news but, as we're being personally monitored, each of us must bear a greater burden and rejoice. Later, take a reasonable amount of money from petty cash and, when no one is around, put it in the handbag of someone who works hard and, more importantly, will announce her good fortune to the world. Decide who deserves the first dose of retribution and at lunchtime cut all the buttons off their coat.

AURAS

You will find it remarkably easy to motivate certain individuals once you have taken them into your confidence and explained that you can see auras, and that their colour and depth of field vary according to the level of commitment they have for whatever they are doing at the time. Say that, in other words, it's a loyalty check. You can now comment, for instance, that a particular aura is looking dark and thin with purple flecks and wispy ethereal bits around the edges. Add that purple is the colour of departure. Start conversations with, "Good Lord, look at the colour of you!"

POLTERGEISTS

Quite simply, damage visitation. Once it has been established that a malign spirit is particularly resentful of the slothful and the lacklustre, and that this manifests itself in furniture being upturned and drawers emptied on to the floor, there will be a startling increase in the levels of stress and commensurate productivity and efficiency. Remember that a completely upside-down desk or, better still, filing cabinet, helps to suggest that super-human strength has been involved.
Health Tip: Remember to lift and drag ergonomically.

CUP CIRCLES

Whether or not anyone believes your story that these were formed in the night by aliens doesn't really matter as the important thing is that no one likes that heat ring left by someone else's tea mug on a nice desk top. Go in early or work late and spend your time wisely by leaving boiling mugs, with wet bottoms, on the desks of all those who will care most. Leave standing for ten minutes and remove to retain the mystery. Leave in place if it's someone's personal mug and you wish to incriminate.

STRESS POINT – Shut Door Policy

Just walk up to someone's office and close the door. Do it several times a day for a week. A deceptively simple action which can have a devastating effect. It creates instant unease and, as a bonus, occasionally traps the claustrophobic. Also, of course, induces anxiety in those concerned about personal freshness.

SPEAKING IN TONGUES

This one can have an impressive effect and should not be confused with Semaphore Tuesday (see page 35).

Practise at home as, to carry it off, you will need to display a heady mix of sincerity and fervour. There will always be disbelievers who will claim you're speaking gibberish, but these will be countered by those to whom it is quite obvious that you have the Holy Spirit within you. Choose one of your more gullible colleagues and tell them you are going into a trance-like state during which you will break the bonds with earth and be elevated to a Nahil Roshaba – or He Who Speaks in Foreign Tongues. Spin around slowly until you get the hang of it and then throw yourself into a dervish-like whirl for a couple of minutes which will be quite a sight for the non-believer to behold. Once you have stopped it will be difficult for you to remain upright so the look of transformation will be reasonably authentic. Even if you collapse on the floor it will look like spiritual exhaustion. Lean on something to stop the room moving and say, "Reh diahub nu rades mella schnaa! Phee demma raik olubas."

I really do recommend that you start using this technique on a one-to-one basis before attempting small crowds where it can be deeply moving and hugely successful. I've witnessed one of my protégés hold her colleagues absolutely spellbound in the company car park – before regrettably hitting her head on a Volvo estate. So, although it requires no equipment, it is not without risk and you should fully rehearse beforehand. My own experience is limited to an occasion where I mistakenly chose to enlighten the entire sales department and found myself so disorientated after my extended whirl (two minutes really should be the limit) that I was astonished to hear my own strange words, became self-deluded and completely forgot I was supposed to be spooking the staff who, rather embarrassed, slowly returned to their desks and left me sitting on the floor next to Belinda's revolving chair.

Never forget when bringing faith and spirituality into the workplace that the challenge is to unbalance rather than unhinge. Although the deranged employee can cause considerable stress in others there is always disruption and time-loss, particularly when emergency services have to be called.

Chapter 7
Conspiracy Theories

The urge to deceive is a creative urge and the ability to stay on top depends on your skill at standing upright with a boot on each of the twin broncos of the business rodeo, Belief and Scepticism.

The expertise to engender faith and cynicism in equal measure, although not entirely compatible with the previous chapter, can be enormously helpful when your company requires a gradual and sustained increase in stress levels, and it can forge an anxiety alloy of remarkable strength. The techniques outlined in this chapter represent current thinking as far as both undermining people's common sense is concerned and also, crucially, replacing it with outrageously ambitious beliefs and goals, which they are too frightened to question.

MOONSHOT MISSIONS (AND OTHER FAKE LANDINGS)

Few rational people now believe that man ever walked on the moon and yet, astonishingly, for many years it was generally accepted as fact, even though neither the technology nor the need existed at the time. But the latter day scepticism has come, not from this knowledge but from the very strength of the belief itself. The architecture of faith is cluttered with conceits and cries out for the austere uncompromising lines of iconoclasm. You will have many opportunities to build an arch of hope and then dismantle it brick by brick to make a folly.

PREPARING FOR THE IMPOSSIBLE

Setting unachievable business targets for departments within your company can have a devastating effect on group morale and so should certainly be a cornerstone of your overall strategy.

Mission Improbable 1

Inform them that the new financial year is one of great opportunity and holds promises of huge reward for the bold, and, in order to secure the future of the company, you have set a budget which is just over double what has been achieved this year. This will obviously involve extra hours and commitment from each team member, which will be amply rewarded by a huge sense of personal pride and team achievement. Give each of them a plastic toy soldier and insist they keep it prominently on their desks as a totem. Explain that it's because they are all warriors and they must hold the figure up and shout, *"Attack!"* each time you walk past them.

Mission Improbable 2

Tell them that the results for the current financial year, ending in two month's time, will almost certainly show a huge downturn in performance and that, unless something exceptional happens in the next eight weeks, the work force will have to be severely curtailed. Look around and say, "However, if any group of colleagues and friends were equipped to deal with this crisis, it is the band of people whose brave faces stare back at me with resolve and fortitude even as

I set them the challenge of their lives. I can feel your strength and determination like a wave breaking over me, and hereby commit myself to matching it in equal measure. Indeed, I will show my renewed confidence in the future by ordering a 2-Season sleeping bag with pillow attachment for each of you, and an industrial washing machine with drier so that none of you need be inconvenienced by trips home for a change of clothing. I promise I shall not profit from your labour and will pass on any discounts I get for bulk purchase of essential foodstuffs. I hereby pledge I will keep floor rents at the pro-rata rate of what our landlord currently charges."

Setting unachievable personal objectives for each individual can have a remarkably deleterious effect on confidence.

Mission Unfeasible 1

Tell the workforce that the company is about to launch a bid for a Belgian company you can't, for legal reasons, name at the moment. However, when it comes off in the next few weeks you will be selecting ten members of staff to be transferred to Belgium and so you insist that everyone learns conversational Flemish and Walloon to business level.

Mission Unfeasible 2

Tell the workforce that the business is about to be bought by an ambitious Korean company who will gradually take each of them back to the industrial area of Seoul for three month's re-training and, quite reasonably, is demanding that everyone learns the language. Reassure them that Korean shouldn't be too difficult to learn as it's linguistically affiliated to Japanese and its orthography has been heavily influenced by Chinese.

NOTHING IS WHAT IT SEEMS

This is a training plan which recently came out of Canada and is premised on research showing that people benefit from being shaken to the core and living in fear of their lives.

Mission Uncomfortable 1

Call the entire company together and, affecting funereal tones, say that what you have to tell them is so sensitive that lives will surely be lost if the secret is not kept. You have learnt that your business, which is badly behind budget, is an integral part of a money laundering operation for the Russian mafia's drugs, sex and illegal arms trade. Sinister figures have taken financial control of the company and you believe that two of their foot soldiers are actually working alongside us! "Yes, standing amongst us at this very moment, which is why we must all pledge out loud and with our hands on our hearts the following. Repeat after me. I swear on my life (they repeat)… that I will remain loyal to the company (they repeat)… and work all hours that God sends (they repeat)… to change its fortunes (they repeat)… and make our Russian Fathers proud (they repeat)."

Mission Uncomfortable 2

Choose the person who most needs a shot of ten dollar tension and cut up letters from headlines in a newspaper to form the words "I LOVE YOU", which you leave on their desk. Maybe a week later you leave "I STILL DO!" Then up the stakes with "WEAR YOUR BLUE SHIRT TOMORROW IF YOU LOVE ME TOO." Then a few days later, "WHY DO YOU HIDE YOUR FEELINGS?" End the correspondence the next week with "YOU MAKE ME REALLY ANGRY." Wait a couple of days and then go into their office, closing the door and asking them if you may speak to them in the strictest confidence. You have now had several phone calls from a colleague of the same sex who appears dangerously obsessed with them. "They keep saying they love you because you're a rebel, you don't take orders, you don't work your cute butt off like the other morons." The only time this strategy has failed me is when the senior figure I was talking to said he knew all along how I felt about him and would I like to go to the cinema on Tuesday and maybe a bite to eat at his place.

Never forget that impossible targets and blind terror are the cathedral and high court of the city of business.

CHAPTER 8
ROLE PLAYING

So many unenlightened companies, still the vast majority of businesses I'm afraid, treat role play as a constructive and creative way to develop an individual and a team. They are deluded even in this simple belief. Research coming out of Vienna proves what we have all suspected for some time: no one but an idiot or a failed thespian enjoys role play. However, had the training companies who have made a fortune out of promulgating this nonsense had the courage and the belief to take it to its limits they would have discovered that role playing can lead to serious disorientation and identity crises which almost certainly results in hypertension and a commensurate increase in productivity.

CLASSICAL MYTHOLOGY

I'm confident that anyone who has read this far will share my feelings for Greek and Roman mythology, and will already know that either of them presents limitless possibilities as far as tension and distress are concerned. Out of the two, and if you only have time for one, I'd go for a Greek for best results. Was it not Aeschylus who gave Prometheus, bound in bonds of iron, pinned by a stake through his chest to a slab of rock at the bidding of Zeus, and plunging down a rift in the earth to be plagued by a daily visit from an eagle to tear his flesh and gnaw his liver, the immortal line: *"O majesty of earth, mother, O sky and air whose encirclement brings light for all to share. See me now, how I suffer these unjust torments."*

I started off looking for a conflict that involved great armies so that all your staff could be involved in terrible battles and could get into the spirit of things. I concluded, as I'm sure you have already, that what your company needs is the Trojan Wars. Not, of course, the bit about the horse, which would be too costly in terms of time and resources to reconstruct, but the nine years which preceded this event. Depending on the needs of your company, you may wish, as I have in the past, to dramatically condense the action. I suggest you stick with Homer and that you popularize by choosing inappropriate people to play leading roles.

- **Greeks** – Achilles, Agamemnon, Ajax, Athena, Diomedes, Menelaus, Nestor, Odysseus, Patroclus.

- **Trojans** – Aeneas, Cassandra, Hector and Andromache, Paris and Helen, King Priam and Hecuba, and the Amazons (choose the little guys!)

- **Gods** – Aphrodite, Apollo, Poseidon, Zeus, and any others you can remember.

If it's a large company and you want some more leading roles then you can of course add the allies of Troy, the Lycians led by Glaucus and Sarpendon.

Each day everyone must be in work one hour earlier and battle must commence immediately. It must cease at the time of a normal day's start and then recommence for the full one hour lunch, regardless of whether anyone is eating or in the cloakroom. Everyone then spends an hour after work continuing their mortal combat. Essentially you have to ensure that everyone knows who everyone else is, including the hordes, and then let them get on with it. There may be the odd minor injury but the vast amount of damage will be done to egos and, more regrettably, to the office environment (emphasize before you begin that damaged equipment must be paid for by the normal user). There will be an incredible and vengeful resentment that may spill over into minor bloodshed, but it will most certainly result in the most pressurized, distrustful and stressful environment you have ever managed to create.

The traditional length for a Greek war is ten years but as I suggested earlier you may feel it appropriate to shorten this time. I usually end with the death of Hector, deserted by the gods, deceived by Athena and slaughtered by a merciless Achilles. A difficult day in the office one could say.

Important note: make sure that you are *always* Zeus and that they all know – even the other deities – that you are the supreme god, and therefore absolutely untouchable.

I was going to spend an equal amount of space on Time Travel and Monsters from the Deep, but I really do believe that the Classics – exemplified by the Trojan Wars – will give your business everything it requires to stay ahead of the competition.

In fact, to encourage you, I'll leave Ancient Greece with *The Iliad* and Achilles explaining to Priam the ultimate reason for human misery:

No human action is without chill grief. For thus the gods have spun for wretched mortals the fate of living in distress, while they live without care. Two jars sit on the window sill of Zeus, filled with gifts that he bestows. One jar is full of evils, while the other holds blessings. When Zeus, delighting in thunder, takes from both and mixes bad with good, a mortal at one time encounters evil, another time meets good. But the one to whom Zeus gives only troubles from the jar of sorrows, this one he makes an object of abuse, to be driven by cruel stress over the face of the divine earth.

STRESS POINT – Role Rotation: the quick way to discomfort

This one is easy to get wrong as you must take into account that jobs have to be done, albeit temporarily, by those not normally doing them, so key functions crucial to the health of the company need to be given to the competent. Apart from that, and let's face it, you're only talking about a couple of people, anything goes – including, briefly, the sanity of the entire office. You can put each job on a ticket and then, working down the telephone list, pick one from a hat. Or, you can pull a name out of one hat and a job out of the other. It's as simple as that, but the pre-draw anxiety coupled with the post-result distress will do wonders for your business. When you're tired of tickets just go round the office like Zeus, clap your hands once like thunder, and point to a mortal: "You, over there," and: "You, come here." A good one for the end of the week.

TIME TRAVEL

I suggest there hasn't been a place in history which hasn't been stressful for its occupants, but pre-history offers all sorts of possibilities for successful role play and personal development. It's the same mandatory rules as before – an hour before work, an hour at lunch and an hour at the end of the day. This is a vigorous game and, managed strictly, will result in three hours of pettiness, chaos and above all, fear. It will be extremely difficult to distinguish Neanderthal Man from early *Homo sapiens*, and they are quite likely to share the same confusion (as they don't have the language) and be attacking their own side anyway! The only ones simple to identify are the sabre toothed tigers who roar a lot, rake the air with bent fingers and often assume the right to leap on prey from office furniture which is quite high. Cautionary tale: **When I was younger I was a purist, and when I instigated my first prehistoric role play I insisted that everyone wore swimming costumes. I urge you from the bottom of my heart not to make the same mistake.**

MONSTERS FROM THE DEEP

Not dissimilar to Time Travel but with less defined roles, I suppose. It's different in that everyone chooses what type of frightening sea creature to be and then displays the attributes with facial expressions, swimmy movements of their arms and disposition to others suspended in the same area of the office. For some strange reason slapping of faces often plays its part in settling disputes over ownership of the seabed and the odd headbutt is not unknown when a large fish is frustrated by a giant octopus.

CHAPTER 9
COLONIZATION THE ROMAN WAY

This is a useful and unusual way to gain total control over the far flung areas of your building. It helps if you acknowledge to yourself that you are a Caesar responsible for the running of a huge empire whose borders you are pledged to expand, or at the very least defend. Keep up the stress by continuing to treat your employees with distrust and disdain, but ensure that some of them believe they have infiltrated your inner circle, where, even if they are not consulted, they will be the beneficiaries of your munificence. In reality, this enables you to give generously of stress.

Look on your employees as rather inferior specimens, savages if you like, who should be grateful for the patronage of Rome and should most certainly pay its taxes and obey its laws. Don't forget that Roman law is the basis for modern civil law and this can be used in your defence if an action is attempted against the hints of slavery you have managed to introduce in spite of the stultifying and misguided labour legislation which protects the innocent and never allows them to reach their full potential.

APPOINTING PROVINCIAL GOVERNORS

An easy way to do this is to take each head of department and elevate them to this position of supreme authority within their domain. For instance, your head of admin would become the Governor of Administration and Gaul who would wield great power and, fortunately for stress levels, probably use it unwisely. If a key member of your team is reluctant to become a governor then you can use Role Rotation (see page 68) to replace them with someone more able to enter into the spirit of things. **There will always be those prepared to betray their colleagues to feather their own nests. Just keep an eye on the over-zealous appointee as your company needs a fully fit workforce, devoid of minor injuries, to take full advantage of legionary stress.**

THE AUTHENTIC ROMAN LOOK

Any attempts I have made in the past to coerce employees into togas and sandals have ended in precisely the type of revolt that a skilled administrator of a province would normally avoid and so I suggest, at least at the start, that you command your governors to limit their ambitions to office layout and customs. These would be backed up, of course, by the strict, uncompromising enforcement of Roman law, the mere threat of which, I have found, can reduce citizens to a jelly-like consistency.

The Roman look for offices is easily achieved and merely requires order, calm and a long straight, seemingly endless pathway between lines of desks. It is always useful to wage a relentless campaign of Stress Points in order to browbeat one of your more spirited colleagues, a potential Spartacus, into such a depth of subjugation that his face is permanently haunted by fear and he looks to the ground as you pass. Then move his desk next to the equivalent of the Appian Way so that travellers may learn the punishments of Rome.

IMPOSING TAXES

Like most modern tax systems you can explain that the levies are being imposed to maintain the infrastructure of the Empire, with the priority spend going on defence and law and order. Your situation will be no different from any other in that the money will actually be spent to dominate, to the point of tyranny, the average law-abiding citizen in each department of your company.

I have found it easy to impose a levy in the past by calling a company meeting and asking who has ever donated to a charity or is pleased that part of their income tax goes to the health service and the defence of their country and its values. I have never had anything less than a one hundred percent show of hands. Tell them that you are pleased to announce everyone will be able to contribute to making their company a better and more secure place to live and that money raised will initially go towards enlarging your office and making it a more prestigious environment for customers and clients so that there will be an almost instant commercial payback for everyone. Emphasize that this voluntary payment is entirely mandatory and select a collaborator, preferably someone obsequious to you but overbearing to colleagues, and put them in charge of the weekly collection. The amount should be small enough to be passed off as fun but will still cause mass seething resentment of almost unbelievable proportions, creating an environment where stress can multiply and prosper.

You must then insist to your principle Governors that they impose tithes on their citizens but allow them to set the level so that, even though the money goes to Rome, they feel they have a certain amount of autonomy. They will soon become deeply hated figures and the increased efficiency in their provinces will reflect this.

Once the tension within provinces is at optimum levels you must order your governors to impose tolls for entry by other colleagues into their province. For instance, someone from the Administration province must pay a tithe to enter the Accounts province. This is a good one for inter-provincial rivalry and it's always interesting to see how full of invective and invention close colleagues can become.

Warning: This one requires the full majesty of Rome and iron-discipline from you to stop aggrieved and sword-wielding colleagues from invading other provinces.

There is something quite beautiful about a well-governed province where a subjugated people emmanate unspoken resentment as acute stress contorts their silent faces. Be careful, though, as I was once asked if, as Caesar, I was above the law, to which I nobly replied, "No." I then spent the next week paying a fortune in taxes every time I left my office.

MOCK EXECUTION AS A LESSON TO THE INNOCENT

This one is actually more difficult than it sounds, as to be totally effective it cannot be done very often, and therefore the victim must be chosen carefully so that an opportunity to completely destroy the nerves of a potentially excellent worker is not wasted. It is important that when you enter their office the ceremonial Legionary's spear you have made looks authentic. Have matching tea-towels draped on either shoulder to look ceremonial. It is important to close the door behind you and say, in a loud voice, *"You have transgressed the laws of Rome and must pay the ultimate price. I am empowered by Jupiter, Supreme God and Prime Protector of the State and my act of justice has been fully authorized by the Senate."* Look them coldly in the eye and show disdain devoid of pity. Briefly, very briefly, place your second hand on the spear and slightly tilt it towards them. Then quickly lean forward to confiscate the huge pen and pencil collection stashed in their pink desk tidy.

A GIFT TO THE GODS

You have now got your company working in a time of numerous deities. It would not be surprising, or unreasonable, for at least one of them to require that sacrificial rites occur somewhere on your agenda for the success of the company. Here's one to turn an adrenalin flow into a raging torrent. Announce Pet Wednesday when everyone's cats, dogs, rabbits, mice and other furry creatures can be brought to work.

Merely by announcing it you'll see the stress levels increase for those who don't like animals and for those who think it will be cruel for them, with the wonderful bonus that there is bound to be someone who will have an extreme allergy to something or other and will probably come out in a severe anxiety rash at the very thought of Pet Wednesday.

When the great day comes you'll find that everyone is understandably excited at the opportunity to show off their favourite furry companion and it will be with a sense of excitement and pride that they all troop down to the dining area (this will help the stress levels of the hygiene freaks too!). You will have deftly hung tablecloths on the wall behind you which, with two hand-made ceremonial spears leaning upright and apart to suggest a doorway, will correctly give the impression of a great temple. You may choose to wear a long bath-robe with a towel on your head for added affect. Stand with your back to the spears and with your hands resting on the dining table you have dragged in front of the temple. Ask for the doors to be shut and unbelievers to be barred from entry. There are many variations on the speech but here is a basic one to help you learn your craft: "Thank you for coming to this holy place in our time of trouble and torment. As I stand at this altar I hold in my hands the cutlery of divination and whatsoever creature they shall point to shall be honoured and chosen to appease the gods and it shall be anointed thus before it begins its journey to the heavens."

Signal to the flautist (well you hopefully found someone with a descant recorder anyway) that the joyous music should begin and, with trembling knife and fork held before you, walk toward the slightly uneasy gathering of man and beast. I don't think I need to continue the instructions. Be confident that the room will empty quickly and with maximum panic and much barking and that the threat of another Pet Wednesday will be enough to keep stress levels at an all time high amongst animal lovers in your company.

STRESS POINT – Disappearing people

Select from the vulnerable but highly talented group the one who you think would benefit most from being completely ignored. You'll see them get tenser and more nervous by the day but will note with satisfaction how their capacity for quality work, already sky high, has rocketed to another planet. Start by refusing to say hello or goodbye and continue by repeating, "Hello. Is anyone there?" if they phone. Don't answer their emails. To make it work properly you really must ignore them. Completely. To the point of not acknowledging in any way their existence. More than once I have sat on a lap in a meeting as, of course, I couldn't see the person concerned, and, on a memorable occasion, I walked into a toilet and bumped into someone halfway through his urinal visit.

It may be appropriate to choose to be a governor rather than a Caesar. I can recall a time of deep distress in my life when, as Julius Caesar, I had, by out-manoeuvring my fellow directors, wrecked the Republic of Rome at board level and, with a genuine sense of hope and pride, established the Empire. It was, of course, now much easier to control the stress levels of my citizens – one of whom, in a well-intentioned joke that went horribly wrong, attempted to assassinate me by pushing me off my chair. Her judgement had obviously diminished as her stress levels had increased (I was suggesting I might send her to another colony – in Richmond as it happens) and the strength with which I was ejected from my chair, with the words "Die, Caesar!" rather took the humour from the situation. Afterwards, the image of Caesar with a plaster on his nose and his left arm in a sling was one which I'm afraid it was all too easy to mock, and my fellow directors, sensing I was at my weakest and emboldened by the masses, took the cowardly opportunity to behave dishonourably. I can't say more on this matter because a final settlement has yet to be reached.

PATRONIZING THE ARTS

Literature, theatre and music were an important part of the cultural mix within the Roman Empire and so you are presented with a unique opportunity to increase stress levels by cultural methods not normally associated with the workplace. You will have established sufficient power to insist that everyone enters a competition in which the best works will be performed after work every Thursday and Friday evening. The Friday is particularly important as it has traditionally been the time when workers begin to wind down for the weekend. If you can't be bothered to have quite so many entries in the competition, you can instruct each department to nominate an individual or group who will represent them in the contest. For example, Finance may choose a poet and Transport enact a small play. It is vital that you use your critical faculties to determine those people who have the most talent and then to reject them immediately.

As Caesar said, "*Give me men who are without talent so that they may agitate the sensitive.*" Do it properly and you will have a great success on your hands with stress levels rising wonderfully on Thursday and Friday and residual resentment fully in place the following Monday. Appalling musical and thespian displays will not only bring ritualistic humiliation to the performers but will give a heightened sense of anxiety to all those forced to endure the endless tedium. And don't forget the painting competition where the winners will be happy to talk at length about their work of art which now hangs proudly on the wall in Telesales. You can encourage them, by clever questioning, to talk for ages on what they feel watercolours give them over oils and how they have managed to master the ethereal qualities of an elusive sky as they point to what, I can guarantee, will look like the work of a fruit-eating chimpanzee in a spitting competition.

You won't be able to operate at this exceptional level for many months and it will soon be time to move on to other strategies and methods for inducing maximum stress, found in this book. It will have been a stimulating time. Have no regrets. All empires return to dust in the end but remember that the Dark Ages which followed the fall of Rome could not eradicate the profound imprint left by Roman Civilization.

CHAPTER 10
SOFTWARE SOPHISTRY

Companies have an almost total reliance on their IT systems. Their employees can have a matching emotional dependence on their computers, with which they spend more time than with partners, and have a closeness and familiarity with their keyboards seldom matched in their relationships.

This almost unhealthy regard for electrical goods must be fully exploited so that the employee is not only lost for work but feels that his or her once reliable computer is now a fickle creature which has begun to spurn the dominant partner.

Important: Most of the exercises below demand high level Screen Raiding, the technique which uses speed, agility and adrenalin to evade detection.

OFF/ON RELATIONSHIPS

This one works really well for those colleagues who are so dependent on their computers that they're reluctant to leave their desks. Make sure that when they return to their machine it is, inexplicably, in another programme. Do this two or three times before going to the next level – switching it off! By now they'll be suspicious so make sure you use advanced Screen Raiding methods when finishing off the exercise by unplugging the thing. If, after several days of this, they are still unhealthily calm and balanced, you must unplug the lead from the back as well and throw it out the window.

Warning: do not cut through electrical cable unless your altruistic mission is to give maximum stress to the person finding your body.

CAN YOU HEAR ME?

This one has limitless possibilities once you have convinced the operator that their computer is writing messages to them when they are out of the room. You can start off with a simple "Hello, where have you been then?" before moving on to "I know what you've been doing." All innocuous enough but warming-up the recipient for a confusing "I can't see why nobody likes you," followed later in the day by "I think you should try a different toothpaste." Once you've reached the "I don't want you to touch me again," stage, you can be as gratuitously unpleasant as the situation demands. Always remember that you are doing this for the good of the individual involved and for the benefit of the company.

STRESS POINT – Turning it around

Wait until they've left the room and turn their monitor around so the screen is facing away from them – as though it's turned its back on the one who loves it. Do this as often as you can to the same person, and no one else, and even if they don't believe their computer is capable of sulking it will certainly drive them round the bend.

EMAILS TO SPREAD PANIC AND ALARM

When you see this one in action you'll wonder why it isn't the most popular method of inducing individual and corporate stress ever! Give it time. You must always use someone else's machine and ensure that the email you send is relevant to that department. For instance, when no one is on reception, nip behind the desk and email the entire company to the effect that Maintenance have said there's a pressure bubble in the plumbing leading to a blow-back and in less than five minutes raw sewage from the outside main-pipe will pour into the office. Please lift any bags or boxes from the floor before leaving the building by the fire exit.

Important: never let your well-intentioned plans to deceive your colleagues degenerate into simple hoaxes which involve police, fire or ambulance services, as, from experience, there can be serious consequences.

A quick and easy one, yet enormously effective, is to send an email from the head of Salaries apologizing that wages will be at least two week's late going into the bank as the company don't have sufficient funds at the moment. Thank them for their patience and say you'll let them know of further developments.

One I haven't tried myself but comes highly recommended is to wait until a top member of the company has gone on a business trip for a few days. Go into their office immediately and send out an email from their computer to the effect that they have been notified by the local health authority (who have refused to name the carrier) that a member of the company has contracted a nasty and highly contagious disease, but is refusing to acknowledge the condition or to accept any form of treatment. Suggest that until the person is identified, it may be advisable to bring in your own crockery and to avoid any physical contact with any other colleagues, including using other people's phones and having face-to-face conversations. By sending an email as though it were the last one before the sender rushed out on the trip, you have ensured that it cannot be exposed as not entirely true for several days.

SPECIOUS SPREADSHEETS AND FALLACIOUS PIECHARTS

Create a spreadsheet at leisure in the comfort of your own office purporting to show that the company's expenditure is currently greater than its income. Email as an attachment to someone who is absent from work at a time when the Finance Director is also away. Yes, you've guessed it! Now email it to the Finance Director and go into his/her office, open the attachment and leave it on screen. I guarantee that within ten minutes the entire company will be worrying about their jobs.

Here's another good one, which is not dissimilar in technique from the exercise above but is more focused on a particular member of staff and his personal stress needs. Create a spreadsheet which purports to show the amount of coffee he drinks in a month, the level of electricity his work space consumes, the amount of time he has spent on personal calls, the amount of time he has wasted during business conversations on the phone, the amount of water he uses, the amount of time he has spent in the toilet and talking in the corridor etc., his weight/work ratio, in fact anything you think will cause him anxiety when you send it to him from the famously absent Finance Director.

Pie charts are more attractive and can be used to show consumption on a department by department basis or can show (quite splendidly in full colour) the consumption of each person within a department. It can cover anything from staples to oxygen but it is normally the level of detail with regard to private habits – sometimes lurid and distressing – which troubles even the sceptics and causes a torrent of fear in the more sensitive and vulnerable.

Chapter 11
Appraising Performance

It has been fashionable, to the immense cost of companies, that most appraisal policies emphasize the strengths and achievements of employees and seem more concerned with morale and the feel-good factor than with addressing the vital needs of both the individual and the business, in order to keep stress levels in line with commercial ambition. I can't state too strongly that there is a paramount need to pull from a company, root and branch, the sweet-blossomed but insidious Tree of Contentment.

ASSESSING AND OPPRESSING APPRAISERS

You obviously can't appraise the entire workforce, so, with almost evangelical zeal, you must assess each of your lieutenants and ensure they use the same assessment methods on their staff. There will be so many positive things they have achieved in the past year, born of genuine hard work and endeavour, that it will be simpler and more constructive to concentrate entirely on their failings, however imaginary they might be. They will then bring this constructive attitude to their own team.

This is Cascade Carbining, whereby everyone shoots the person below them (obviously they're all merely wounded otherwise it doesn't work).

ESTABLISHING THE FAILURES

This is easily done for even the most perfect of employees, as, despite their rarefied level of performance, everything is relative. All you have to do is pick on and pull to bits the achievements which were merely fantastic rather than brilliant. At this elevation your worker, as well as being enormously efficient and effective, will probably be an artist and visionary and so will have all the prerequisite sensitivity to render him vulnerable to even the mildest hint of criticism. Take this into account before giving him the full onslaught of your surprise, anger and dismay at such a dismal and lacklustre performance from a key member of the team.

Once you have dismantled and distressed the Perfect, it will be an even simpler matter to destroy the confidence and up the stress levels of the Very Good Indeed.

EMPHASIZING WEAKNESS

Once you have highlighted the professional inadequacies of the person being appraised, you must never stop and give them time to respond before you move on to complete the picture of embarrassing failure by listing their personal inadequacies in both habit and appearance. I always advise protégés that, when trying this for the first time, they should have prepared a list so they can read from it in an accusatory fashion, thus avoiding having to make it up as they go along. The latter does have its attractions but I've found there can be a tendency, in a moment of uncertainty, to repeat the insults from the previous appraisal session. It was entirely inappropriate to call someone fat, bald and stupid, as I did once, when the young woman in front of me quite obviously had all her own hair, and, to my astonishment, was quite prepared to show how fit she was by leaping up and breaking my spectacles with a swift right hook to the head.

> ## STRESS POINT – Dealing with competence
> This is always a tricky one in that you need to gently shake them from their equilibrium in a sensitive way, without disturbing their output. The method I favour is to go in wearing the rather smart cap of a naval captain and say,
> *"Seriously, if this was an ocean going liner you'd have disappeared over the side two miles out of Southampton. If I was Nelson I'd make you walk the plank and if this was a pirate ship I'd leave you on an island to rot. Let's talk again next week."*

THE APPRAISAL AS AN INSTRUMENT OF TORTURE

Some people stubbornly continue to remain unstressed, however much invective is levelled at them over a sustained period, and the performance appraisal is, providing you have time, an exquisite opportunity to induce the type of mental anguish most commonly associated with the very heights of artistic and creative accomplishments. You may wish to wear your black suit for this one and, after shutting the door and saying that any cries for help will not be heard, you can begin by telling them they have made you very unhappy indeed. Very, very unhappy. And even if it takes all day you are going to get the truth from them as to why they have personally let you down and betrayed the company. Make sure you have left careful instructions that when your coffee is brought in to the room, there is to be no eye contact, and the appraised will be not offered any drink at all. Not even water. Especially not water.

AVOIDING THE POSITIVE

Sometimes in the midst of dark ruin and despair, a shaft of light will fall and a flower will blossom. You must tread on it immediately. There will be occasions – I've had them myself – where, however carefully you have engineered the appraisal, the victim spots an opportunity to make a verbal escape by rapidly listing all the genuinely positive things they have achieved over the previous year. You can avoid this dangerous outbreak of hope by picking up your papers and leaving the room.

Always remember that the simplest way to avoid the positive is to cut short the meeting.

CHAPTER 12
MEETING DYNAMICS

Internal meetings whether regular or ad hoc, at whatever level in the company, afford valuable opportunities to increase both individual and group stress. Discomfort and Doubt are the Twins of Insecurity and you must pay attention to detail to make sure they fully come into play. Quite obviously you start with a room which has as little natural light as possible, windows that can't open and with a temperature inappropriate for the prevailing weather. Then the seats must be hard, with modern and strangely shaped backs. Once physical discomfort has been firmly established, you should start making attendees uncomfortable with the atmosphere, the agenda and, if not too impractical from a business point of view, with the conclusion.

ARRANGING A MEETING

The first thing to alter is the time of the meeting, Start in advance by changing the day and, as it draws near, continue by constantly – I suggest at least once a day – altering the time. Always be at least half an hour late when the time arrives but every so often be early and show your agitation that others have cut it a bit fine.

It is important that you make at least three changes to the venue so that it may first be planned for the board room, then someone's office and finish up in the small meeting room. Obviously don't inform everyone who is planning to attend of these changes.

For the inconvenience of others you should always endeavour to change the purpose of the meeting and, if this fails, you must definitely change its name into something more meaningless.

Never forget that at least one wholly inappropriate person should be invited for their own consternation and for the general confusion of the meeting. The most I've got away with is three in a meeting of eight, but, in a moment of divine inspiration, inviting a bike courier in reception to join a board meeting as independent observer has perhaps been my greatest success. I remember it was followed by a rather good lunch at which he was a great hit, a phrase rather too apposite in that, as we decanted from the building, he enthusiastically peddled into the back of the chairman staggering towards his Bentley.

STRESS POINT – Size Seating

As they walk into the meeting room instruct staff to stand next to one another with their backs to the wall before rearranging them in order of height (xylophone style) without, of course, telling them what you're doing. Then sit the smallest at one end of the table followed by the next short arse, etc. When all are seated, start the meeting immediately. Once you've mastered this simple exercise you can arrange the next meeting by weight, smartness, ears, ugliness, whatever you like. Hairstyles, from sensible to ludicrous, always works well but, as individuals have to slowly rotate, this one requires more time for judging.

PREPARATION

It's absolutely vital that you make no preparation for meetings at all. This allows you to express astonishment that others have not come fully prepared with briefs and suggestions.

If you feel the urge to prepare then you must arrive heavily over-armed with statistics and reports so it's a bit like Arnie as The Terminator, pump-action shotgun in hand, visiting the Bournemouth Debating Society.

I strongly recommend that the only preparation you make is to surreptitiously remove from the screen of a presenter, prior to printing, a key phrase, and the concluding paragraph, or really I suppose as much as you have time to do without risking being caught. Sabotage is an exhilarating thing when inflicted on a rival who you know will, as a result of the increased pressure, come out of it a stronger and more worthy adversary.

If you don't have the time or the opportunity to change their documents then I urge you to remove at least two pages from the master set waiting to be photocopied.

MEETING ETIQUETTE

This must be fully acknowledged so that you know what you have to undermine. You know your colleagues and their weaknesses and predilections so I'll leave it to you to decide on the most inappropriate behaviour. Inane remarks are always a useful way to throw someone off balance and repeating them simply adds to the pressure. If someone actually has the gall to play to the gallery by saying something equally ludicrous then you must insist that her remarks are minuted.

It's always useful to misread body language so that for instance if someone briefly catches your eye you should, if physically possible, slide your foot under the table and rub their shoe. If you can't reach them just wink and mouth a subtle but unmistakable little kiss towards them. This is particularly effective if they are of the same sex or there is a huge difference in age. Be warned that in my experience, seriously misreading body language and reacting in kind can lead to distressing circumstances in which you can find yourself the innocent recipient of inappropriate emotional attention.

SPEAKING

Rather ironically, I find that not enough attention is given to Target Talking in meetings. Yes, people speak but you haven't come for a conversation, you're there to stress up your colleagues and get them performing. Use words economically and make sure they always hit home. However, ensure you've practised talking over someone, which is a brilliant stresser, before you do the real thing.

The effects of random acts of misplaced unkindness cannot be overestimated. Choose the least deserving individual, someone who has prepared for the meeting and has already made a valuable contribution, and then begin the elegant but difficult technique of Phrase Lobbing. This involves putting words in other people's mouths, or, by deliberately faltering, encouraging them to finish your sentence and then ridiculing what they have apparently said. This technique is wasted on a one-to-one level and should be reserved for larger meetings so that public humiliation can take full effect. You must never feel guilt. Remember the words of Voltaire: "A life with stress is a horse without wings."

MAKING MEETINGS INTERESTING

This one can be really enjoyable but is not an indulgence as it will lead to misunderstanding, confusion and annoyance, all of which are great contributors to a company's good health. It's a form of unwitting role playing, with you being the only person in the room who knows what characters you have allocated to everyone else. In the following example, these characters are farm animals.

Look on the room as a farmyard and decide who is to be which animal for the duration of the meeting. Don't tell them but make sure you consistently respond as though they were that animal.

So, when the horse makes a point, you might reply with, "Whoa there fella, don't you kick back now, we don't want to be saddled with a problem!"

When the sheep has finished talking you could say, "I'm sorry but you keep repeating what others have said."

Once the cow has stopped you respond with, "You're always looking for new pastures when we should concentrate on key functions and milk them for all they're worth." (You can even play the bull and tell her she's a service industry.)

Once the hen has finished cackling you can dismiss her with, "I think you're implying that it's a chicken and egg situation."

After the duck has stopped quacking you retort, "Look, you're being over-cautious, once we're in the swim we won't have to dive for cover."

As soon as the goat has stopped his bleating you dismiss the argument with, "You're being negative again. There are far too many buts in your life."

The sheepdog's point may be particularly obtuse in which case you will be happy to point out that, "Once more you're barking up the wrong tree which is frankly a trial for all of us."

After the donkey has stopped braying reply with, "I regret to say you've just made a complete ass of yourself," before adding, ambitiously, "It's a situation that can't be eeyored." Trust me, no one will notice.

The pig should obviously be told in no uncertain terms to "Stop squealing and trot out last month's figures one more time."

The cat at some stage will surely be caught "undeservedly lapping up the praise before going into another flap."

When the goose stops honking it's time to say, "Calm down, you're being over-protective."

Keep that lot going for two hours and you will deserve all the stress you get!

Chapter 13
Between A Sponge
And A Soft Place

We are talking leadership! Nothing else. There are no tough decisions, just people too weak to take them. You must have the ability to see everything as an easy option. Celebrate the fact that the business world is divided into choices and opportunities, and that stress will help you with both. Look at your staff. They need direction, they need energizing and, above all, they need stress. Within any organization there is an opportunity to gain the high ground – a time when the bold climb from the ledge of mediocrity to scale the ridge of opportunity before racing along the plateau of tedium, leaping across the chasm of uncertainty and landing in the high and verdant pastures of success. Do it! All you need is the confidence gained from the knowledge that everyone else lacks it. The thing that equips you to make a decision is the inability of others to take one.

You can re-invent yourself as soon as you choose. Just go in to the office as normal one day. Stop at the door, tuck your trousers in your socks and affect a silly run with your arms out and your head at an angle. Shout that you cycled the 20 miles to work, painted a picture in the night and, in a visitation before dawn, was given second sight by a shamen from Ilford. They'll accept it. But what a wasted chance. If you do that, then you're not yet ready to become the Stressmeister!

No, you must go to the office tomorrow or the next day and make a difference. No one will stop you, because you've re-invented yourself as capable of achieving anything for your company. You are Renaissance Man – Leonardo's geometric figure, with your hands and feet in everything. You will take total control of the insignificant and excel in crisis management and revel in your ability to maintain it.

Use the methods I've described, confident in the knowledge that you will see your company gain a competitive edge so sharp it will cut through the lacklustre cant of your rivals who appear more concerned with the welfare of their staff than whether any of them will have jobs in twelve month's time.

Remember, identify the colleagues who will benefit from isolation and rejection and instil in them a sense of paranoia before giving them positions of authority where they can be a positive influence on the health of your company.

Give your very best workers pointless jobs, send them on demeaning training courses, start needless arguments and constantly question the obvious. See obstacles as stimulants while you use demotion as an incentive and language as a means of confusion. As I said earlier, a thriving business, like an ancient empire, will only prosper as long as its ambitions and its aggression are matched by corresponding levels of stress.

Don't allow contentment, let alone happiness, to creep its insidious way back into your company. If people are pleased with the job they have done, it is your duty to disabuse them of their smugness. Satisfaction is the quick route to company malfunction. Remember, anxious people produce answers.

Stress them up! The Stressed shall inherit the Earth!

THIS BOOK IS REVERSIBLE AND CAN BE READ
INSIDE OUT BY THOSE WEAK-WILLED, MISGUIDED
INDIVIDUALS WHO APPARENTLY BELIEVE THAT THEIR
COMPANY WILL PROSPER BY PURSUING A SO-CALLED
ENLIGHTENED POLICY WHICH ENCOURAGES TEAM-
BUILDING, TRUST AND HAPPINESS IN THE
WORKPLACE.